Colors in Nature

Blue

Lisa Bruce

Raintree

Chicago, Illinois

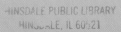

Printed and bound in the United States at Lake Book Manufacturing, Inc.
07 06 05 04 03
10 9 8 7 6 5 4 3 2 1

Library of Congress Cataloging-in-Publication Data:
Bruce, Lisa.
  Blue / Lisa Bruce.
      p. cm. -- (Colors in nature)
Includes index.
Summary: A simple introduction to blue things found in nature.
  ISBN 1-4109-0724-4 (lib. bdg.) -- ISBN 1-4109-0729-5 (pbk.)
  1. Color in nature--Juvenile literature. 2. Blue--Juvenile
literature. [1. Blue. 2. Nature. 3. Color.] I. Title. II. Series:
Bruce, Lisa. Colors in nature.
  QC495.5.B58 2004
  535.6--dc22

                            2003015282

Acknowledgments
The publishers would like to thank the following for permission to reproduce photographs: pp. 4, 5 Sinclair Stammers/
Science Photo Library; p. 6 Christer Fredriksson/Bruce Coleman, Inc.; pp. 7, 8, 9, 18 PhotoDisc/Getty Images; pp. 10, 11
KPT Power Photos; p. 12 Geoff Bryant/Science Photo Library; pp. 13, 20 Corbis, pp. 14, 15 Nature Picture Library; p. 16
J. L. Mason/Ardea; p. 17 Kim Taylor/Bruce Coleman, Inc.; p. 19 ImageState; p. 21l Lynda Richardson/Corbis; p. 21r
Richard Hamilton Smith/Corbis; p. 22 Robert Harding Picture Library; p. 23 Peter Evans

Cover photograph by PhotoDisc/Getty Images.

Every effort has been made to contact copyright holders of any material reproduced in this book.
Any omissions will be rectified in subsequent printings if notice is given to the publishers.

Some words are shown in bold, **like this.** You can find out
what they mean by looking in the glossary on page 24.

Contents

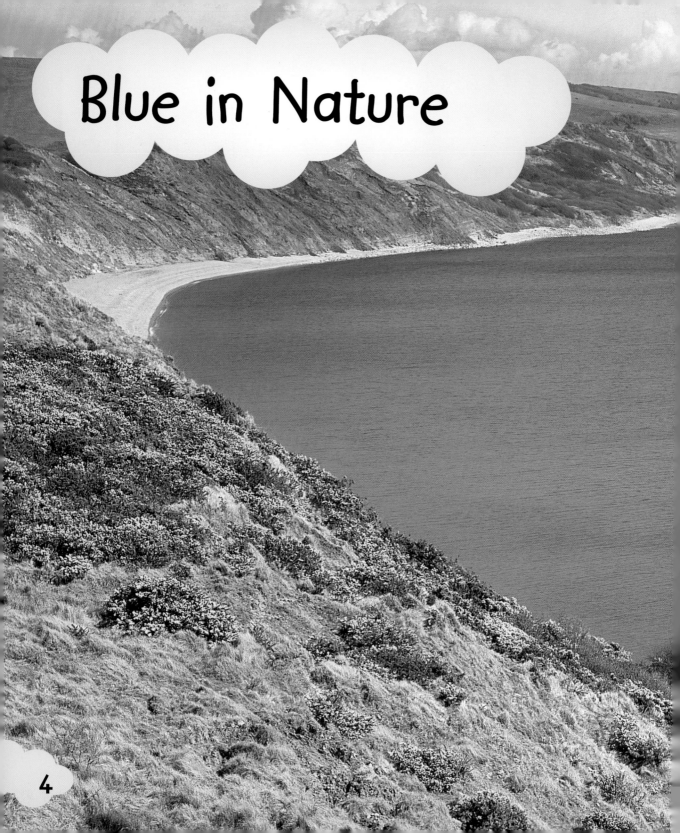

Blue in Nature

There are lots of blue things in nature.

Where in the world can you see blue?

5

Blue Flowers

Lots of flowers are blue.

These daisies are blue.

Bluebells have tiny blue flowers.
They look like a blue rug in the woods.

7

Blue Sky

On some days the sky is light blue.

On other days the sky is bright blue!

Blue Water

Rivers and lakes sometimes look blue.

The ocean sometimes looks blue, too.

Blue Animals

This is a blue
whale in the ocean.

Blue whales are the biggest animals in the world.

Blue Birds

Some peacock feathers are bright blue.

Kingfisher feathers are blue, too.

Blue Fish

This **tropical** fish is shiny and blue.

These **neon tetras** are blue, too.

Blue Bugs

This blue bug is called a **damselfly.**

These blue bugs are called bluebottle flies.

Blue Food

blue cheese

blueberries

Here are some blue foods.

blue potatoes

blue corn

Have you eaten any other blue foods?

Changing Color

On a cloudy day the sky is gray.

The sun comes out.
The color of the sky changes to blue!.

Glossary

damselfly (You say DAM-zuhl-fly.) Kind of insect that looks a little like a dragonfly

kingfisher Kind of bird that lives near ponds and that dives to eat fish in the water

neon tetra tiny, shiny fish that people keep in aquariums

tropical place where the weather and ocean water stay warm all year

Index